I0159266

Talk to Me! Listen to Me!

Keys to Improve Communication and
Questions to Deepen Relationships

Carol McCormick

American Council on Exercise
Certified Personal Trainer
Certified Health Coach

Celestial Press
New York

Talk to Me! Listen to Me!
Copyright © 2014
Carol McCormick

Cover photo of people © Depositphotos.com/DragonImages

All rights reserved. No part of this publication may be reproduced, stored in a retrieval system, or transmitted in any form or by any means—electronic, mechanical, photocopying, recording, or any other—except for brief quotations in articles and reviews, without the prior permission of the publisher.

The author is a certified personal trainer and a certified health coach through the American Council on Exercise. Even though ACE is internationally recognized as one of the top fitness organizations in the world, neither she nor they are qualified to dispense medical or psychological diagnosis. Therefore, this book is not a substitute for the professional psychological or medical diagnosis or treatment of a psychologist, psychiatrist, or physician. Readers should consult appropriate healthcare professionals for the diagnosis and treatment of any psychological or medical conditions.

ISBN-10: 0967536847
ISBN-13: 978-0-9675368-4-2

Books by Carol McCormick

I'm Hungry! I'm Bored!
Eat and Play Your Way to Better Health, a Leaner Physique,
and a Happier Life!

The Missing Piece
Award-winning Inspirational Love Story

Your Special Gift
A Preteen Primer to the Facts of Life

Window Pains
Modeling Positive Behaviors

CONTENTS

OVERVIEW

When thoughts and feelings are expressed during deep levels of communication, true intimacy is established and attachments are formed that are virtually unbreakable. Today, we see more and more people interacting electronically rather than enjoying face-to-face or side-by-side conversations. As a result, rather than feeling more connected, people often feel more disconnected than ever.

Talk to Me! Listen To Me! is as a tool to help turn things around. Although this book is a short read, it will take days, to weeks, to possibly months to implement, since the latter questions take time to emerge, develop, and unfold. The more thought-provoking questions may also run into chats that last for hours, either because of the time it takes to reveal the answer, or because the answer may lead to even more questions and deeper discussions.

The questions can be chosen cafeteria style from the light and fun, to the more weighty and serious. They can be used during one-on-one situations or in groups such as classroom settings, college dorms, orientations, sorority and fraternity interviews, and even in corporate team-building meetings.

They may also be used as a quiz type game, or as an icebreaker at parties, or as a "get to know you" handbook while dating or making new friends. They can be worked through with a companion, a relative, or a spouse to deepen existing relationships. A couple may also choose a few of the more provocative questions to answer while on a weekend retreat.

Talk to Me! Listen to Me! is an excerpt from the full-length book, *I'm Hungry! I'm Bored!* This special edition contains the entire chapter, "Deepen Your Relationships," with additional information and over fifty more questions than the original.

COMMUNIQUÉ

The majority of people's problems are caused by the fact that
they are disconnected with the rest of creation.
C.S. Lewis

You hear with your ears, but you don't really listen.
Isaiah 42:20

Communication to a relationship is like oxygen to life. Without it, it dies.
Unknown

You never know when a moment and a few
sincere words can have an impact on a life.
Zig Ziglar

If only someone would listen to me.
Job 31:35

Actions speak louder than words.

1

TUNE IN

As you know, communication is an exchange of thoughts, feelings, and ideas between two or more people. I'm sure you also know that it's not just what is said, but *how* the words are said and how they are received that determines whether the relationship is thriving, floundering, or nonexistent.

Defining communication is not the problem. Most people know what it is. Making strong personal connections is the difficult part, because not everyone knows how to do it.

Some people think there's a magic trick to making a friendship or marriage work on a deep and lasting level. They buy the latest magazines with lofty promises emblazoned on the covers: "Make Him Only Have Eyes for You," "Secrets to Winning Her Heart," "Recipes That Will Have Him Eating out of Your Hand," or "How to Spice up Your Marriage." You know. You've seen them. Great stories, I'm sure, but without a deep level of communication, these actions often lack the strength to tighten *emotional* ties.

Communication is so important that it was the first subject taught on planet earth when humans came to be. Math whizzes and science geeks eventually came on board and had their place, but in the beginning, life was all about words and learning to express what needed to be said.

Communication is the foundation of all business ventures and close relationships. If you look at the origin of the word intercourse (Medieval Latin, 1425-75), you will see that it meant then, and still means today, an exchange of thoughts, feelings, and communication between individuals or groups of people. It wasn't until 1798 that the term was included to mean the sexual act itself in addition to the previous definition. In both cases, linguists equate the two meanings to that of bringing individuals closer together.

Open and honest communication reveals a person's soul, to help us understand, to empathize, to enjoy, and to create a tie that binds one human being to another. This is especially true when done on a personal level while in a person's presence.

A major problem that arises from screen-to-screen communication is that when texting or tweeting the meaning is often misconstrued, because physical signs are missing that would be obvious if speaking in-person. By listening to the tone of voice and observing body language, the following statement is easily understood, but when the same words are texted or tweeted, they are more difficult to decode. They may even take on a whole new meaning.

For example, let's say a co-worker sent this text to an associate after an intense business meeting: *"I can't believe you did that!"* The person receiving the text has no idea whether the statement is one of elation or disdain. One meaning says that he's amazing. The other could mean he's a jerk. Without hearing the tone of voice, or seeing the facial expressions or body language, a person often has no way of knowing the sender's intent.

The more our senses are involved in a conversation, the more a person is able to determine what is really being said. Aside from the above-mentioned clues, there are sighs, groans, pauses, hesitations, inflections, fluctuations, and cracks in the voice that all come into play when interacting with another person, *while in that person's presence,* or while speaking *directly to a person* even when they are not in our presence, such as when talking on the phone.

Texts, tweets, and posts often omit obvious and subliminal cues that we would normally gather while conversing in-person. This is why they conjure up confusion. Wait too long to reply, leave out that little smiley face, or simply answer with a "k," and you may have started a war without even knowing it. All because there is no tone of voice to hear or body language to behold when chatting screen-to-screen.

Silence also speaks volumes if we look and listen for veiled messages that tell us something more is going on than what is being said. Management consultant, Peter Drucker, believes that the most important thing in communication is hearing what isn't said.

The old adage, "Reading between the lines," is really just being an intuitive listener and an observant people reader. Those who are in tune with others often perceive hidden thoughts, agendas, and emotions that go undetected by the average listener.

Authenticity and vulnerability are also necessary to cultivate a relationship. True connection comes when laughter, thoughts, ideas, and feelings are shared heart-to-heart, one-on-one, or in small groups. This act of being knit together in love and unity is one of the most vital links to lasting fulfillment and lifelong friendships.

Genuine communication must also have a focused listener. I'm fascinated by the fact that the word *listen* and the word *silent* contain the exact same letters, but in a different order. This interchange often reminds me that in order to truly listen, I must learn to be silent. I may offer a nod or two, or a few mutters of acknowledgment, or a brief question or comment, but other than that, listening is all about focusing on what is being said and noticing behavioral cues in the other person.

We see an example of this direct attention when observing dogs that are raised and trained solely to bring comfort by "listening." Comfort dogs are sent to areas that have been hit with crisis situations, to provide unconditional love by doing nothing more than offering their quiet presence and tender affection to traumatized survivors.

Sometimes people simply need a listening ear to hear them when they speak. Quiet companionship is often more healing than well-intended words of advice. The following suggestions and questions may help improve communication and deepen your relationships.

2

DEEPEN YOUR RELATIONSHIPS

When I was fifteen years-old, I went to the lake with a group of my friends and then decided to go into the water while they stayed on the beach. I didn't know how to swim very well, but I knew how to float on my back, so I foolishly assumed that I would be okay. After a few moments of drifting atop the gentle waves, I stepped down, but barely touched the sand with the tip of my toe, so I panicked. And then I bounced. Up and down, on my toe, while lifting my chin as high as I could and raising my hand in the air. On the third bounce, my friend saw that I was in distress. Mimi quickly jumped into the lake and brought me safely to the shore. Even though I never went completely under water, I believe that without her help this could have been a tragic situation.

My friend was not only "there for me," but she took action when it was needed. Back on the beach, we went about our business like nothing had ever happened. We didn't talk about it, report it, or analyze it. She didn't boast about her rescue, or reprimand me for making an unwise move. And we never brought the incident up again until later on in life.

People need a trusted friend when they're on the throes of drowning. A listening ear to hear without condemnation. Someone who loves them enough to teach them to swim, or to pull them back to solid ground when they are struggling to keep their head above water or to merely stay afloat.

3

THE BUDDY SYSTEM

The following questions are divided into three sections that move from shallow to deep levels of communication. Some of the questions are meant to be fun, while others have the potential to deepen existing relationships or mend those in need of support or repair. Many of the questions are frivolous and silly, while others are more thought-provoking and may even provide a measure of emotional healing.

The latter questions may also help those who feel overwhelmed to keep them from drowning in anger, frustration or feelings of hopelessness. If you plan to work through this list with a friend, family member, or significant other, the questions should be asked in the *group order* listed in order to build trust. Some of the "Wading off Shore" questions can be asked to younger children for fun without continuing on into the deeper waters.

If a person feels uncomfortable answering any of these questions, he or she should be given the option to "pass." The participants can also set out on a solo voyage of self-discovery with pen and pad in hand to answer the questions alone.

The "game" begins as a silly quiz or interview, but gradually becomes more in-depth with the purpose of helping the child or adult become more open and self-aware. This insight allows the person to emerge and grow toward his or her fullest potential.

I encourage you to ask only a few questions at a time, but then ask one or two more questions in addition to the original one, such as, "How did (does) that make you feel?" or "What can you do about it?" or "What is it about that one that you like so much?" to keep the conversation rolling.

This open dialogue can strengthen family connections or tighten bonds that are already in place with a friend. This interview is meant to be played with *both* people taking turns, asking questions, and exchanging answers, so there will be *equal sharing time* for each person. This shared knowledge provides leverage to those who have dared to open their hearts and expose their thoughts, dreams, and even their wounds, since the other person has also done the same.

This shared information also helps ensure that there will be no emotional harm done via gossip or online social chitchat, since both participants are making themselves open and vulnerable. When this deep level of camaraderie is established, the friendship often becomes stronger. This mutual unity creates a protective wall to shield, support, and guide those involved, as they venture out into an ever-changing and oftentimes harsh or confusing world.

Are you ready? Here we go…

4

WADING OFF SHORE

In this section, the conversation begins with causal questions that lay the foundation of trust. Wading off shore is a safe way to test the waters before playing in the deeper waves. If the answers to these shallow questions are met with anything but utmost acceptance, the person will learn not to reveal deeper thoughts in the future.

1. What do you like to collect?

2. What is your favorite sound?

3. What was your first real job?

4. What is your favorite flower?

5. What is your favorite movie?

6. When do you feel most alive?

7. What is your favorite smell?

8. Who inspires you to do better?

9. Who or what makes you smile?

10. Have you ever had a nickname?

11. Who do people say you resemble?

12. What song best describes your life?

13. What does your dream home look like?

14. What person do you admire the most?

15. What do you like best about your life?

16. What is your favorite outdoor activity?

17. What is your favorite month or season?

18. What is your favorite family tradition?

19. What do you think needs to be invented?

20. What is your favorite quote from a movie?

21. What is the best book you've ever read?

22. Describe a typical weekday in your life.

23. What is your earliest childhood memory?

24. What was your favorite subject in school?

25. Have you ever won a contest or an award?

26. What does your dream vacation look like?

27. Have you ever broken a bone or had stitches?

28. What would you like to be doing in five years?

29. What skill or talent do you wish you possessed?

30. What is the first thing you notice about a person?

31. What is the most unusual job you have ever done?

32. If you won $1,000,000 what would you do with it?

33. If you could have one superpower what would it be?

34. What is the most beautiful sight you have ever seen?

35. Which animal do you wish you could be for one day?

36. If you were a car or a truck what kind would you be?

37. Who is the most famous person you have ever seen or met?

38. Which school teacher do you remember the most?

39. If you could go anywhere in the world, where would you go?

40. If you had one wish, what would it be? (Besides more wishes.)

41. What is the most memorable scene from your favorite movie?

42. What is the most unusual or funny thing your pet has ever done?

43. Who has made you laugh more than anyone else? Describe a situation.

44. What was your first impression of me? (The person asking the questions.)

45. What is the funniest thing that has ever happened to you or to someone you know?

46. If you could spend one day with a famous person from the past or present, who would it be?

47. If your house caught on fire, what would you grab as you ran out the door (besides a person or pet)?

48. If you were stranded on a deserted island, what is one thing that you would want to have with you?

49. If someone wanted to make a movie about your life, what actor do you feel would best play your part?

50. When you were a child, what did you want to be when you grew up?

5

PLAYING IN THE WAVES

Most people don't naturally "open up" about serious issues in their lives because they are afraid others may criticize or simply not like them. Yet it's often helpful and healing to do so, given the right circumstances in the presence of a caring listener.

Life is a lot like writing a novel. It's only when the reader sees the characters' weaknesses, strengths, flaws, phobias, and virtues that they care about them. Those who enjoy a good story will often root and cheer, and even grow to love the underdog, or the tormented hero, or the waif who is cast aside. *This peek into the hero or heroine's heart and soul is the key to making the reader care about them.* If the characters were perfect or stoic or wore emotional armor, there would be no tale to tell. The challenges and struggles are what make the story a page turner. Without conflict and resolution, or trials and triumphs, a novel often flops.

Even though this is true in the literary world, most people are hesitant to reveal their innermost thoughts. Because of this, the person asking the questions should make a vow of confidentiality to ensure trust.

The promise should sound something like this: "I want you to know that you mean a lot to me, and you can talk to me about anything. No matter what you tell me, whether good or bad, I will always care for you, and I will never share what you say with anyone else, without your permission."

Your verbal guarantee may give the person courage to speak freely. This openness of thoughts and feelings may also help the child or adult emotionally heal, if needed. Playing in the waves is an easy way to become accustomed to deeper water. These questions are a bit more personal, but many are still breezy and fun. The same rules apply.

51. What is your pet peeve?

52. What do you dread doing?

53. What is your greatest strength?

54. What is your favorite love song?

55. Who brings out the best in you?

56. What do you feel that you do well?

57. What do you believe about God?

58. What do you believe about angels?

59. What is your definition of success?

60. How do you want to be remembered?

61. What do you see when you daydream?

62. What is at the top of your bucket list?

63. Who do you look up to as a role model?

64. What do you like to do in your free time?

65. What do you wish you knew how to do?

66. What is your favorite inspirational quote?

67. What book has influenced you the most?

68. What movie have you seen multiple times?

69. What is your most embarrassing moment?

70. What is your happiest childhood memory?

71. What one word describes your personality?

72. What words or motto do you try to live by?

73. What is the best gift you have ever received?

74. When do you feel that you became an adult?

75. When have you felt the most safe and secure?

76. What mistake or hardship taught you a lesson?

77. What song makes you happy when you hear it?

78. What person or situation makes your heart pound?

79. What would you do if you knew you couldn't fail?

80. How would you describe your closest relationship?

81. What is the most difficult thing you have ever done?

82. What is the best advice someone has ever given you?

83. What event in history do you wish you could have witnessed?

84. What do you admire about your mother or your father?

85. What is the most daring thing that you have ever done?

86. If you could relive one month of your life, when would it be?

87. What legacy would you like to leave after you are gone?

88. What surprised you the most when you became a parent?

89. What is the craziest thing that you have ever seen someone do?

90. What are the most meaningful words that you have ever heard?

91. If you could accomplish anything in the world, what would it be?

92. If someone wrote a book about your life, what would the title be?

93. What words of wisdom would you give a teenager?

94. What is the most romantic true love story that you have ever heard?

95. What are five random facts that most people don't know about you?

96. What is one thing you know you'll regret if you never get to do it?

97. If you could change anything about yourself or your life, what would it be?

98. What quality do you possess that you hope your children will someday possess?

99. If you were going to lose one of your senses, and you had the ability to choose which one, what would it be?

100. When you think back on your life, what do you wish you would have done differently?

6

SWIMMING IN THE DEEP

When swimmers feel secure after playing in the waves, they may be more inclined to venture into the deep, if a faithful friend is there for support or to teach them how to swim. The simple question of "How did that make you feel?" often has the potential to open a flow of emotions that have been buried in the deep.

When this emotional gate is open, it is best to be shockproof and just listen, or ask a few non-intrusive questions without offering advice. If you show any sign of sudden surprise, or offer unheeded counsel during a sensitive or hot topic, the gate often slams shut and the conversation ends.

When a child or adult feels free to reveal his or her heart to another person, their words often become the catharsis that siphons off hot or toxic emotions, so healing and restoration can begin. If the unhealthy emotions happen to be directed toward you, it is best to just sit and listen while nodding in agreement with an attitude of acceptance, until the person has finished venting. Defending yourself at this point will also shut the gate and the conversation will end (or flare up).

Your silence does not necessarily mean that the child or adult is right and you are wrong. You are merely acknowledging and respecting his or her right to *feel* as they do. When the person has finished speaking, you may need to ask for clarification or forgiveness, and then ask what you can do to fix the offense or improve the situation. And then by all means, do your best to make amends and take the steps to restore the relationship. Once this has been completed, a floodgate of positive and healthy emotions often begin to emerge.

When you begin this level of swimming in the deep, it's best to set the stage. Profound questions are often easier to answer when a friend or family member is facing *the same direction* as the person asking the questions, such as while sitting on a porch, deck, or patio loveseat in the evening by moonlight, candlelight, or solar lights; or while sitting side-by-side in front of a fire-pit or campfire; or while riding together in a car on a road-trip, especially in the evening. A similar scenario can be arranged on a park or piano bench, or while washing and rinsing dishes together. There seems to be less intimidation in answering personal questions when both people are facing the same direction, particularly in subdued lighting.

If you are trustworthy, shockproof, and non-judgmental, a person will tell you almost anything. Ask questions that will help them find answers, rather than voice your opinion, unless, of course, they ask for it. The following questions have the potential to evoke an array of emotions ranging from laughter to tears. Therefore, the one asking the questions should also be prepared to listen with empathy and sympathy, along with confidentiality.

You may also want to rephrase the person's answer back to him or her in a gentle tone of voice to let them know that they've been heard. This is similar to what drive-thru restaurant servers do when they repeat your order back to you. This paraphrasing also confirms that you understood what they said.

For example, Sally says, "I felt like I was invisible." Joan then *softly* says, "You must have felt so all alone." Instantly, Sally feels understood and the emotional gate inside her heart opens up a little bit more.

The reflective response reassures Sally that she has been heard, and it helps her feel safe and accepted. As a result, she is more inclined to continue sharing her thoughts and emotions as the conversation continues.

A few casual questions are interspersed with the serious ones to give the swimmers time to exhale.

Ready? Take a deep breath.

101. When have you felt the most loved?

102. What was a pivotal point in your life?

103. When was the best day of your life?

104. When was the saddest day of your life?

105. What is your greatest accomplishment?

106. What is your biggest regret?

107. What do you worry about the most?

108. What fear would you like to conquer?

109. What makes you different from everyone else?

110. What is one struggle that you have overcome?

111. What is one struggle that you have yet to overcome?

112. If you could do anything in your life over again, what would it be?

113. What would you miss most if I was not a part of your life?

114. Who has inspired you to become a better person?

115. What do you believe about the afterlife?

116. Have you ever wanted to run away? If so, why?

117. How are you like your mom or your dad?

118. What are the best ways to demonstrate love?

119. What deed have you done that created a ripple effect?

120. Who is the most courageous person you know, or have ever heard about in history?

121. What would you like written on your tombstone someday?

122. What is the hardest part about growing up (or being a parent)?

123. What do you wish you could say to someone who has hurt you?

124. What do you wish someone who has hurt you, would say to you?

125. What is the kindest thing that anyone has ever done for you?

126. What is the kindest thing that you have ever done for someone else?

127. What has someone done that made you love them more?

128. What is the greatest lesson you learned while growing up?

129. What has someone done that made you respect them more?

130. What would you like to do for someone else if you had the money and time?

131. What were your family dynamics like when you were growing up?

132. What question would you ask your parents if they had to be completely honest?

133. What makes you feel the most loved?

134. If you could bring someone back into your life for one day, who would it be and what would you say to him or her?

135. If you were stranded on a desert island and only five people could be with you, who would they be?

136. What do you hope to accomplish in your life?

137. Who do you find hard to forgive?

138. What do you believe is the most important thing in life?

139. What song makes you feel sad when you hear it?

140. Who do you wish you were closer to?

141. How do you know that I love you (or care about you)?

142. What is the hardest thing you have ever done?

143. What is the scariest thing you have ever experienced?

144. What is one deed that you wish you could delete from your past?

145. If you had twenty-four hours to live, what would you do?

146. What three people have made a difference in your life?

147. What do you see when you look in the mirror?

148. What do you wish people knew about you?

149. If you could make one phone call before you died, who would you call, and what would you say?

150. What is something you would love to do but lack the courage to do it?

Wouldn't you feel valued or cherished if someone took the time to ask you these questions and then listened to your answers with heartfelt interest and empathy?

A bond is not only formed between the person asking the questions and the person answering them, but studies have also shown that emotional healing often takes place when someone feels that he or she is completely *heard, understood,* and *unconditionally accepted* by at least *one* person. One person! Amazing.

Overall health and mental health thrive in this type of environment and healing often spills over into the physical realm too, once the soul is opened, loved, and protected under this cloak of camaraderie.

7

LIFE PRESERVERS

Years ago, there was a show on television called *The $64,000 Question*. The game was played like many of today's competitive shows, where the questions become more difficult as the contestants progress to the next level. While $64,000 may not seem like a lot of money compared to shows like *Who Wants to be a Millionaire*, it was a lot of loot back in the 1950s. Answering all the questions correct had the potential to drastically change the player's life.

The following question will not necessarily make you rich, although it quite possibly could in the future, but it is meant to discover where your passion lies, to buoy your life and other people's lives for good. This passion has the potential to make you rich *inside,* as you *enrich the lives of others.* These meaningful deeds deposit true wealth internally and eternally.

The $64,000 Question

> What is something you love to do, something you could do for hours on end, even if you weren't getting paid for it, but felt that by giving your service away it would *benefit other people*?

Simply put, what makes your heart go pitter-patter? What lights your inner fire of desire when you think about making a difference in the world? Once you have the answer, ask yourself: ***What is the first step I need to take to begin moving in this direction?*** The answer to this question has the potential to become a life-changer for you, and a life-preserver for other people.

In order to live a meaningful life, you must do meaningful deeds. Take the plunge!

* * *

Thank you for reading *Talk to Me! Listen to Me!* I hope that you enjoyed it. If you found this book helpful, please consider posting an online review so others may benefit too.

You may also enjoy the full version of the 250 page book, *I'm Hungry! I'm Bored!* Many ideas and examples for the *$64,000 Question*, are also suggested in the *I'm Bored!* section, along with other fun, educational, and productive activities.

I'm Hungry! I'm Bored!
Eat and Play Your Way to Better Health, a Leaner Physique, and a Happier Life!

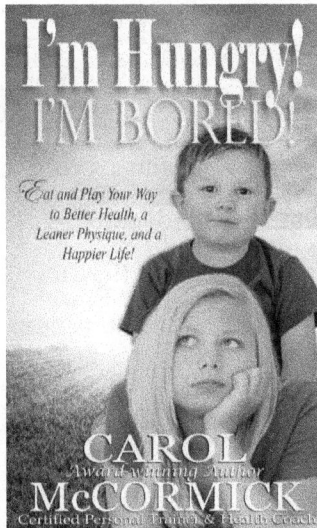

I'm Hungry! I'M BORED!

Eat and Play Your Way to Better Health, a Leaner Physique, and a Happier Life!

CAROL McCORMICK
Award-winning Author
Certified Personal Trainer & Health Coach

For Adults and Tots Through Teens

www.carolmccormick.com

TABLE OF CONTENTS
(Condensed version)

I'M HUNGRY!

I'M BORED!

I'm Hungry!

PRE-GAME WARM-UP

"I'm Hungry! I'm Bored!" How many times have you heard these words from your children? Those who are old enough to take care of themselves usually do so by raiding the fridge or ransacking the cupboards, or by flopping down in front of a PC, TV or other electronic device for hours. If your children are young, you have more of a say in their eating habits and their time spent with the one-eyed-cyber-monsters. Older kids, now that's a different story. The task becomes a tug-of-war, because teens don't always listen or want to do what's best for them. Not only that, but there's the added challenge of competing with their friends who may sway them from your good intentions and influence.

Well come a little closer. I've got good news for you. *I'm Hungry! I'm Bored!* can help your children make better food choices and encourage positive behaviors by making meaningful activities and good nutrition enjoyable, fun, and exciting.

This book will arm you with hundreds of ideas that can help your child thrive in life. Because a child left to himself, when it comes to food, activity, and entertainment, will often take the path of least resistance and choose junk food to eat, or the internet to occupy his time, often because he or she doesn't know what else to do. The children who do know their options will still need additional ideas, examples, and encouragement to hoof the higher path on the oftentimes bumpy road of life.

That being said, I present to you a virtual goldmine of goodies. You hold in your hands, hundreds of hours of gathered facts from credible sources, along with a few gems of my own, condensed and funneled into one treasure chest for easy reading and access.

I've done the footwork for you and provided the *what, why*, and *how-to* of nutrition and weight loss by defining the problems, offering solutions, and then presenting guidelines to carry them through. The *I'm Bored!* section offers hundreds of links and suggestions to great books, movies, places to go, things to do, questions to ask, jobs to perform, and services to volunteer, all-of-which help develop the intellect, confidence, and feelings of fulfillment and well-being. Many of these ideas may also deter the hand-to-mouth eating habit that often accompanies boredom.

<u>End of Preview</u>

If you would like to read more of *I'm Hungry! I'm Bored!* please visit www.carolmccormick.com   or any online bookstore. Thank you.

www.ingramcontent.com/pod-product-compliance
Lightning Source LLC
Chambersburg PA
CBHW060643030426
42337CB00018B/3430

* 9 7 8 0 9 6 7 5 3 6 8 4 2 *